DATE DUE			

Also by William Irwin Thompson

The Imagination of an Insurrection: Dublin, Easter 1916
At the Edge of History
Passages about Earth
Evil and World Order
From Nation to Emanation
The Time Falling Bodies Take to Light

BLUE JADE
FROM THE MORNING STAR

*An Essay and a Cycle of Poems
on Quetzalcoatl*

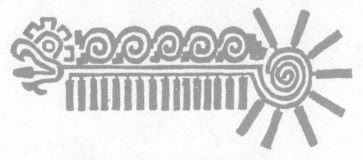

William Irwin Thompson

The Lindisfarne Press
West Stockbridge, Massachusetts
1983

Published by The Lindisfarne Press
R.D. 2, West Stockbridge, MA 01266

Some of these poems have appeared before in *Corona* and *Re-Vision*.
For permission to republish, grateful acknowledgement is here made.
To my colleagues in the Lindisfarne Fellowship, Wendell Berry and
Kathleen Raine, I wish to express my gratitude for their helpful
criticism in preparing the manuscript.

Cover illustration adapted from *Book of the Gods and Rites and the
Ancient Calendar*, translated by Fernando Horcasitas and Doris
Heyden. Copyright 1971 by the University of Oklahoma Press.

ISBN: 0–940262–03–7
Library of Congress Catalog Card Number: 82–84052

Printed in the United States of America

For W.T. Walton

 CONTENTS

THE FLIGHT OF THE SERPENT

Of Quetzalcoatl history knows little, of Quetzalpetlatl, nothing. As "elder sister" and consort of Quetzalcoatl in the mysteries, she appears in the *Annals of Cuauhtitlan* simply as an expression of his fall. On the surface she appears to be a traditional male perception of the female, a perception of the female as the physical body into which the male spirit falls in drunkenness and unconsciousness. In this fall of the celibate high priest into human sexuality is a reflection of the fall of the evening star under the earth where it remains until it emerges from its journey as the purified morning star that prepares the way for its father sun. And in this fall into sexuality is also an echo of the fall of the eternal and unlimited spirit into a mortal and animal body.

These Gnostic themes of "Fall, Sinking, and Capture,"[1] are ones which I have explored before in *The Time Falling Bodies Take to Light,* and this book of verse can be considered to be a second volume in a series. In the first volume I tried to set down the philosophical foundation for a radically different vision of history; here I am trying to move upward from the foundation to an expression of architecture. This is not to say that the first volume should not be seen as *art*, or the second volume as *scholarship*, but it is to say that I have worked very consciously to change the relationships between art and scholarship in the new genre of *wissenkunst.*

Thematically, it is a natural progression to move from a discussion of Ishtar and Gilgamesh, or of Isis and Osiris, to Quetzalcoatl and Quetzalpetlatl. Quetzalcoatl is the serpent that turns into a bird, Quetzalpetlatl is the caterpillar that turns into a butterfly; in both cases we are presented with an image of transformation, of a movement from earth to air, from matter to spirit.

The plumed serpent is, of course, not unique to Mexico. The staff of the god Mercury, the caduceus, is the most familiar image from the classical world of Greece and Rome, but this religious hieroglyph goes back even further to Egyptian culture. A winged snake can be found on the inside of the sarcophagus of Wennepher (380 B.C.), now housed in the Metropolitan Museum of New York. And it would seem that the Hellenistic period, with its proliferation of mystery cults and its passion for religious syncretism in the post-Alexandrian era, was a time, much like our own, of fascination with the occult and the esoteric. The myth of the phoenix seems to have its roots in this Graeco-Egyptian culture, and the myth of the phoenix presents many striking similarities with the myth of the plumed serpent. The quetzal bird is said to make its nest only on the top of trees in the full light of the sun. The serpent that has turned into a bird thus has to make its way up the trunk of the tree to move out of the dark into the light. And so it is with the phoenix, for it is said to have once been a lowly worm that fed in the dirt, but then as it slowly made its way up the trunk of the tree, it began to become transformed into a bird. Once on the top of the tree, it no longer ate the gross food of earth but the more refined nectar of flowers and rare essences of herbs. Here in its nest atop the tree it created its own funeral pyre and was transformed into flames, but from the matter left behind, the ashes, another phoenix was born.

Since a quetzalcoatl is a snake which turns into a bird,

and since at least one historical quetzalcoatl is said to have burned upon a funeral pyre, with his ashes rising up to become the morning star, it would be a simple matter to see both the myth of Quetzalcoatl and the pyramids of Mexico as having been inspired by direct cultural contact with Egypt. But it would be too simple. The religious iconography of bird-tree-snake is almost universal. Here, for example, is the legend of how Tai Chi Chuan was invented in ancient China:

> According to the legendary story, Chang San-feng, in the house meditating at noon, heard an unusual noise in the courtyard. Looking down from his window, he saw a snake with raised head, hissing in challenge to a crane in the tree above. The crane flew down from the pine tree and attacked the snake with its swordlike beak. But the snake turned its head aside and attacked the crane's neck with its tail.[2]

In watching the movements of snake and bird, the Taoist sage was inspired to create the contemplative art of Tai Chi. The fact that the monk was meditating under the sun at high noon when he was called to this vision of movement, should alert us that a good deal of information is being presented in the legend.

In the first volume of this series I attempted to show how this complex of bird-tree-snake could be traced all the way back to the upper-paleolithic period,[3] and that wherever this complex appeared, whether in Tantric yoga, or medieval alchemy, or Renaissance Rosicrucianism, it appeared in the context of an esoteric school of contemplative practice. Anyone who has been trained in these techniques of meditation would instantly recognize that what is being presented is an imagistic representation of the nervous system as it is affected during the

various stages of esoteric practice. Today everyone has
seen movies in which a snake charmer from India plays a
flute and causes a hooded cobra to arise out of a basket.
The practitioner of yoga, however, knows from experi-
ence what it feels like to listen to the sounds of the magic
flute of his spinal column, and then observe a force ap-
pear out of the base of his spine, rise up the spinal col-
umn, and then fan out across the brain to flow into a
point in his forehead at the root of the nose. When
knowledge is stored in images it can survive for a very
long time, for stories are literally forms of cultural
storage. But when the esoteric meaning and practice are
lost, the image suffers from what Whitehead called "mis-
placed concreteness," and so we end up with the snake-
charmer performing his art for the tourists outside luxury
hotels. A much more diabolical form of misplaced con-
creteness occurred in pre-Columbian Mexico. In the
religion of Quetzalcoatl, one not only learned how to
teach the serpent how to fly, but how to open one's heart
to the light of the sun. The opening of the heart chakra to
the light is one of the sublime religious experiences, and
this image was used, and is still used today, by the Sufis
as the *insignium* of their practice. The Aztecs, however,
perverted the ancient practice, reduced it to a funda-
mentalist literalism, and began to rip open the chests of
sacrificial victims so that the priest could hold the heart
up to the sun.

The tragedy of the Aztec perversion still lingers on
today, for I have heard highly educated people say to me:
"How can you be so interested in the religion of ancient
Mexico, when all that mysticism led to such incredible
human torture?" It is as if one were to blame the massacre
at My Lai in Viet Nam on Thomas Jefferson. It is, in part,
to help to correct the popular misconception that the

Aztecs are all there is to the history of Mexico, that I felt motivated to put together a more coherent and artistic narrative of the legends of Quetzalcoatl than can be found in tourist pamphlets or the celebrations of blood-lust in the famous novel of D. H. Lawrence.

In each of these cultural contexts in which bird-tree-snake is found, it appears to be deeply rooted in that culture and not an exotic import from some other culture. But as different as the local legends are, what is not changing in these stories is a symbolic representation of the nervous system as it relates to meditational practices. No doubt it is precisely because there are experienced initiates of these practices in these different cultures, whether it is in China, India, Egypt, Europe, or Mexico, that the deep meaning remains the same, while the local illustrations change. There were no quetzal birds in ancient Egypt or India, but there was an understanding of what science would now call "the three brains of man."

> Man finds himself in the predicament that Nature has endowed him essentially with three brains which, despite great differences in structure, must function together and communicate with one another. The oldest of these brains is basically reptilian. The second has been inherited from lower mammals, and the third is a late mammalian development, which in its culmination in primates, has made man peculiarly man.[4]

The old reptilian brain is the snake; it is the brain of the instinctive, the unconscious, the depository of millions of years of evolution. The second brain is the limbic ring, the mammalian brain of "fight or flight," of emotion and a highly developed olfactory sense as a way of perceiving the environment. This limbic ring is the nest of the bird, phoenix or quetzal. The third brain, the neo-cortex, is the bird, the creature of the higher realms of thought. The twin hemispheres of this brain are the two wings at the top of the caduceus, the sign we still see today as emblem of the medical profession.

Now the reason these three brains are symbolically emphasized in various esoteric schools of religion is that as soon as one moves out of the conventional life of society into the mysteries of the temple, he or she undergoes a spiritual evolution in which the evolution of the nervous system is re-experienced in a form of recapitulation. When consciousness is focused with unwavering attention, the body responds. Most often this is encountered in negative terms through a psychosomatic disease in which the symptoms chosen are symbolically rich for the patient. In other cases, either in hypnosis or ecstatic trance, the individual can stop his blood from flowing as he pierces himself, or a saint can develop the stigmata. The symbol is a mediation between the world of consciousness and the world of matter, and if symbols are used in intense practices of visualization, then the whole body, and not simply the mind, becomes involved.

In the first stages of contemplative tantric practice, the instinctive life is energized and one feels an enormous amount of physical and sexual vitality. In men this is experienced as the phallic stage, and one should realize that all the phallic imagery used in the ancient iconographies of Greece, Egypt, or India is not simply referring to fertility and copulative sexuality. During this stage of earthly energizing, the practitioner is counseled not to identify with or act out these sexual energies. Celibacy is the rule. If the rule is followed, and if the contemplative practice is continued, then the serpent begins to climb the tree of the spinal column. In this second stage, the second brain, the mammalian brain, is energized. It is a time of raw emotion and ancient senses. One's passions begin to be wildly intense, fits of crying take one over without obvious cause. Long buried and repressed childhood emotions explode to the surface, and the sense of smell begins to challenge the supremacy of sight as a way of interpreting the world. One begins to smell "auras" rather than see them. One begins to know and respond to people instantly, the way a dog would: lovingly wagging one's tail at this stranger or barking angrily at another. And at this stage too, the student is counseled not to identify with or act out what he is feeling. It is a dangerous time, for the physical and psychic energies can make the individual appear to be quite charismatic, but if the individual involves others in his shifting and unstable fantasy life, then great confusion and suffering can be experienced by more people than simply the student. Jonestown is one of the more extreme examples of the dangers of this second stage.

The third stage is the stage of the bird. In the place where the three brains come together, "the place where three roads cross," is the place of integration, the traditional "third eye." "For the eye is the light of the body, and if thine eye be single, then is thy whole body filled with light." (Matthew 6:22) After years of focused concentration and visualization practices, the third eye opens and the student shifts upward from a physical body to a body of light. The mode of thought shifts from a linear one of sequential words and thoughts to a hieroglyphic one of multi-dimensional geometrical figures or crystals that are at once musical and mathematical forms: it is as if two Bach fugues were being played at right angles to one another. Plato's world of forms and Sufi angelology begin to take on a whole new level of reality.

Now, just as there is a shadow side to the second stage,

a stage that is caricatured in Jonestown, so is there a shadow side to this third stage. The shadow form could be called "paranoid-schizophrenic cosmic synthesis." The hieroglyphic mode of thought is isomorphic to, but not identical with, "schizophrenic word-salad."[5] In these psychotic cases certain traumatic experiences have crushed the ego, and the being is rawly exposed to altered states of consciousness without any yogic training whatsoever. In other cases, through drugs or moments of evanescent artistic rapture, the individual slips out momentarily into another mode of thought. In James Joyce's *Finnegans Wake,* or in Dylan Thomas's sonnets "Altarwise by Owl Light," schizophrenic word-salad is used (not expressed) to force the reader to transcend his normal, habitual, linear modes of language and thought. Shakespeare long ago noticed that "the lunatic, the lover and the poet are of imagination, all compact." But the difference that makes a difference between the artistic genius and the lunatic, or between the yogi and the lunatic, is that the lunatic is in a condition of acute agony, suffering, and existential terror, whereas the other is in a condition of stable, balanced, and creative joy. The paranoid organizes his entire universe around his central dread; his chaos is transformed into one gigantic, coherent, and cosmic conspiracy. He, and only he, has discovered "the secret." And here too is another aspect of the shadow form of the third stage: the cosmic inflation of the ego. A contemplative in a monastery or esoteric school knows that he or she is simply one of a long line of contemplative practitioners, stretching back from the present into the mists of prehistory. And if the monk or nun begins to get a little overenthusiastic about his divine mission in life, the abbot is there to remind him or her to sweep the floor and clean the toilets. Ultimately, the third stage must be a return to the first.

And the end of all our exploring
Will be to arrive where we started
And know the place for the first time.
....
When the tongues of flame are in-folded
Into the crowned knot of fire
And the fire and the rose are one.[6]

When the fire at the base of the spine and the rose at the top of the spine are one, then there is neither snake nor bird, but a feathered serpent. Then the energies of the earth and the energies of the sun can be brought together in a harmony that makes a high civilization possible, for these energies are not simply personal. Social activists have criticized the seventies, with its fascination with Eastern religions and "New Age" mysticism as the narcissism of the "Me Generation." And these criticisms would be well deserved if all there was to teaching the serpent how to fly was simply an almost auto-erotic fascination with one's own central nervous system. But there is a whole other level of meaning to the myth of the feathered serpent.

Both the bird and the snake have evolved from a common genus: one went down into the earth to crawl, the other went up to the trees to launch into the sky. When the bird takes up the snake and flies to the top of the tree, as is pictured in the flag of Mexico, a civilizational ideal is being expressed. Esoterically, there are two human races: one has fallen to the ground and become so entrapped in the body that it can no longer remember its divine origin. The other race is human, but not in what we recognize as a body, and it is seeking to help us up into a consciousness of the spirit. Like Isis, this race is seeking to gather up the pieces of the dismembered Osiris to re-establish their divine marriage. The religion of Quetzalcoatl is anything but a narcissistic concern for the *me*. One needs to remember that the temple of Quetzalcoatl is in the center of one of the largest and greatest cities of antiquity, Teotihuacan. The myth is essentially a vision of civilization, and the pathos and tragedy of the story is that in the battle between civilization and savagery, savagery won the day.

And so there are at least three levels of meaning to the hieroglyph of the feathered serpent that we need to keep in mind. The snake is the earth, and the bird is the sun; the feathered serpent is the world in harmony with heaven, an earth sculpted into a "Pyramid of the Sun." The snake is the fallen human race; the bird is the bodhi-sattvic race; the feathered serpent is the human race in the condition of enlightenment. The snake is the archaic brain; the bird is the neo-cortex, and the feathered serpent is the religious initiate who has consciously moved from physical to spiritual evolution.

Now just as Nazism was the perversion of the high culture of German Romanticism, so the mystical militarism of the Aztecs was the perversion of the earlier religion of Teotihuacan. The political liberal of today grossly distorts and misunderstands history if, in rejecting the Nazis and the Aztecs, he feels compelled to reject all of German Romanticism, all of Mexico, and anything that smacks of mysticism.

One reason that the Aztecs are often confused with the earlier Mexicans in the common North American mind is because of the presence of certain self-punishing techniques in even the pre-Aztec religions. In prayer and meditation, the penitent would pierce his flesh with maguey thorns. When these pre-Columbian practices joined up with the forms of penance and self-flagellation in Spanish Catholicism, an extreme form of Hispanic Christianity emerged in the movement of the *Penitentes* of the Southwest. Because these forms of religious excess are instantly and viscerally repugnant to the Protestant sensibility of a Northern European culture, the cultural polarities repel one another. The Latin person sees the Northern European as locked into a bourgeois, shop-keeping materialism in which he has sold his soul for the mess of pottage of technology. The Northern European sees the Latin as a religious psychopath and is confirmed in the path of cleanliness and technology. And so each passes over the other in mutual misunderstanding.

Precisely because of these misunderstandings, it might be useful to distinguish two different approaches to religious transcendence. All religious techniques attempt to relate the part to the Whole, to show the individual that there is more to existence than a full belly or a full bank account. If we define the *ego* as an aggregation of habits, appetites, and roles pressed upon the growing person by the collective, then we can say that the function of religion is to connect (*religare*—to bind) these fragments with the One, to transcend fragmentation and alienation through Wholeness. But if the *ego* is in a state of aliena-tion and forgetfulness, how can one re-mind it to connect it with the Universal Mind?

Religions through the millennia have chosen a thou-sand different ways, but there are basically two different polarities along which these ways arrange themselves in a magnetic field. There are those techniques that work *against the grain* of animal life, and those techniques that work *with the grain*. The Jewish seder, the Christian eucharist, the Quaker meeting, these are religious forms that accept the animal life and seek to remind us of the Whole through acts of physical food-sharing, commu-nion, and quiet attunement to the individual in the group in a spiritual society of Friends. The techniques that seek

19

to work against the grain are those that frustrate the habitual and instinctive life of the *ego* in order to force it out into the open, into the larger world of Being. If the animal seeks to avoid pain and seek pleasure, then the technique forces it to confront pain. If the animal seeks to be slothful and full of sleep, then the technique seeks to enforce exhaustion and lack of sleep; this strategy is also useful in forcing the dream life into the waking state, and thereby working to effect a new union of unconsciousness and consciousness. If the animal seeks to eat, the technique demands that it fast. If the animal seeks sexual satisfaction, the technique demands that the student simply observe the sexual excitation without moving into the release of orgasm. If any one of these techniques is followed to its end, then the *ego* simply cannot survive, and the individual either experiences a psychotic break, or passes through the initiatory fire into illumination.

Religious techniques that choose to work against the grain of animal life are clearly dangerous; they more often form the way of the shaman, the yogi, the solitary hermit. One need only recall Grünewald's painting of St. Anthony in the Desert to see what the dangers are. Now sometimes the student who has chosen the path of the shaman looks down on those techniques that work with the grain, and this is the trap of Luciferic pride. It is important to emphasize that the techniques that work against the grain are not superior to those that work with the grain; they are simply different. A Quaker in a meeting of the Society of Friends can go as far as or farther than a yogi in a cave in the Himalayas; only an adolescent foolishness would glamorize the path of the shaman or sorcerer, after the fashion of the *wissenkunst* of Carlos Castaneda.

But from the legends of Quetzalcoatl it is abundantly clear that his was the path of the yogi on top of the mountain in solitary meditation. From the piercing with thorns, to the ritual celibacy with his spiritual "elder sister," to the self-immolation by fire at the end, it is clear that the path of at least one of the Quetzalcoatls required working against the grain of normal life. In the *Annals of Cuauhtitlan* there are definite indications that esoteric practices are being alluded to. For example, when Quetzalcoatl places himself in a funeral crypt and stays there for four days, he is not simply invoking the period of time in which the planet Venus remains under the earth; he is engaging in a practice that has to do with the subtle bodies. When the subtle bodies are disengaged from the physical body, the psyche undergoes an initiatory test in the "bardo realm." If the test is successful the initiate returns to the physical body, which all this time has been in a comatose state, in a healthy and sane condition. The initiate has thus won mastery over death and can "die" or disengage the physical body at will. In the more familiar cultural context of Christianity, this is the esoteric dimension to the story of Christ's "Harrowing of Hell." When, therefore, the story speaks of Quetzalcoatl's burning by fire at the edge of the sea to become the morning star, we should not interpret this as a conventional suicide.

The text is quite specific at this point, and through a play upon words it involves other levels of meaning with the death by fire. The Nahuatl scholar John Bierhorst says that there is another translation possible for the line: "the heart of the quetzal rose upward," and that is: "the inner part of the precious penis rose upward."[7] The inner part of the penis, the seminal *prana*, is, of course, the very heart of Tantric practice and the *raison d'être* for celibacy. If the inner part of the penis is rising upward to become the morning star, then we are being presented with a descrip-

21

tion of Tantric illumination as the apotheosis of Quetzal-coatl. Clearly, one of the most important parts of a story is its ending; it is the *telos* toward which the whole narrative is moving. If in one's interpretation of the story, one cannot make any sense of the inner part of the precious penis rising upward to become the morning star, then one had better go back to the beginning and search for another interpretation. If one rejects the religious dimensions of a myth, which seems an absurd thing to do with a religious myth, but agnostic scholars and critics do it all the time, then all one sees is primitive gibberish that confirms the critic in a feeling of civilized superiority.

Another indication in the myth of Quetzalcoatl that esoteric knowledge is being referred to arises with the presentation of the *nahual*, the heavenly double. The concept of the heavenly double was a major feature of Gnosticism; here is Professor Jonas's explanation:

> It symbolizes the heavenly or eternal self of the person, his original idea, a kind of double or *alter ego* preserved in the upper world while he labors down below. . . . Applied to the messenger or savior as it is here and elsewhere, the conception leads to the interesting theological idea of a twin brother or eternal original of the savior remaining in the upper world during his terrestrial mission.[8]

All of which is a rather exact description of the *nahual* of Quetzalcoatl, his heavenly twin Xolotl, who remains above while Quetzalcoatl descends into the world of the dead to rescue humanity. The double is not exclusive to Gnosticism, however, for there is the concept of the *daena* in Persian Zoroastrianism, and Socrates referred at his death to a *daimon* which gave him instructions throughout his life, and it is this Western notion of the *daimon* that W. B. Yeats took up and elaborated in his *A Vision*.

Now with the presence of winged snakes, pyramids, and Gnostic expressions of doubles and the entrapment into the body by the dark god, one might be tempted to see the religion of Quetzalcoatl as a brand of Near Eastern syncretism brought in by transoceanic contacts with the Phoenicians, but that too would be too simple. It is, of course, a matter of the one true faith in Mesoamerican archaeology to insist that there were never any pre-Columbian contacts between the Old and New Worlds. Anyone who dares to suggest otherwise, as have recently Professors Cyrus Gordon and Barry Fell,[9] is dismissed as a crank babbling of lost continents and flying saucers. Personally, I have no difficulty with transatlantic or transpacific contacts, but the religion of the Feathered Serpent goes back even further than the main commercial activities of the Phoenicians and can be found in the earliest Olmec sites.[10] In these murky depths of myth and prehistory there is not light enough to prove anything; or, in another way of stating the problem, there is darkness enough to prove everything. Consequently, what one *sees* is simply a projection of what one *is*. The scholarly narrative is a construction that supports one's own world view. If one is a Theosophist, he sees that both Mexico and Egypt are derivative from an earlier Atlantean culture. If one is an agnostic in a university department, he sees all religious interpretations of religion as the projections and wishful thinking of unscientific cranks and religious nuts, be they Mormons or hippies, Theosophists or New Age Gnostics. When one is dealing with a legendary figure like Quetzalcoatl, Pythagoras, or King Arthur, there is simply no scientific way to settle the matter once and for all. Fortunately, in the world of poetry, as opposed to science, one is not required to prove that Mallory's King Arthur is truer than Tennyson's. Each author is free to offer to the tradition an individual variant of the collective myth.

Quetzalcoatl is even more of an elusive figure than King Arthur, for there is not simply one Quetzalcoatl, but several. Whenever a charismatic leader would reach a certain level of religious or political authority, he was referred to as a Quetzalcoatl. At the time of the Spanish conquest when monks like Fray Bernadino de Sahagún were trying to piece together from their native informants the old history and legends, they were dealing with a situation in which the traditions had not simply been destroyed by the conquistadores and smallpox, but also by the Aztec kings like Itzcoatl who had burned the old glyphic books and replaced them with an imperial version of Aztec history and religion. So what we have in the *Florentine Codex* are fossils and fragments from many historic levels all jumbled up together. There are some individual leaders, like Huemac, who I think are decidedly not avatars of the Feathered Serpent, but simply war lords dressed up in the old religious symbols whose meaning they can no longer fathom. It is as if a Mexican bandit by the name of Jésus were to be confused centuries from now with the original Jesus of Nazareth. Since my interest in the Quetzalcoatl myth is focused on the inner religious vision of the story, Huemac-Quetzalcoatl for me is like eighteenth century graffiti on Stonehenge: it is not part of the essential mystery, and so I simply ignore it.

There are, of course, limits to what one can change, and within these limits in Part One, I have kept fairly close to the texts of *The Legends of the Sun*, the *Florentine Codex*, and the *Annals of Cuauhtitlan*. But before I could even begin to retell the stories in verse form, I had to sort out in my own mind all of the different Quetzalcoatls.

The archetypal pattern that I see expressed in the myth is the ancient Egyptian one made famous by Vico:

> Two great remnants of Egyptian antiquity have come down to us. One of them is that the Egyptians reduced all preceding world time to three ages; namely, the age of gods, the age of heroes, and the age of men. The other is that during these three ages three languages had been spoken, corresponding in order to the three aforesaid ages; namely, the hieroglyphic or sacred language, the symbolic or figurative (which is the heroic) language, and the epistolary or vulgar language of men employing conventional signs for communicating the common needs of their life.[11]

For each of these three ages there is a distinct avatar of the Feathered Serpent. First is the age of gods in which Quetzalcoatl is no mere human figure but a true god who gathers up the remains of the human race after the flood and struggles to re-establish humanity in a new age, the age of the Fifth Sun. Second is the Quetzalcoatl of the age of heroes, the great high priest of Tollan described in the *Florentine Codex*. Here I would agree with Laurette Séjourné that Tollan is not the more recent and militaristic Tula of the tenth century A.D., but the more ancient and sacred ceremonial center of Teotihuacan.[12] This second and more incarnate form of Quetzalcoatl is the culture hero who brings the arts of civilization to his adopted people. He is the mysterious bearded white man from the East. He is the tragic hero deceived by the atavistic sorcerers who seek a return to the prehistoric darkness before Quetzalcoatl's age of enlightenment. Third is the Quetzalcoatl of the age of men, "Our Dear Prince," Ce Acatl Topiltzin Quetzalcoatl, a more solidly historical figure from the tenth century A.D. in Tula.

Topiltzin seems to me to be the leader of a revitalization movement who tries to block the power of the warrior caste by resisting human sacrifice and seeking to restore the ancient religion of the Feathered Serpent. Like many other prophetic leaders of nativistic movements, be they Moses, Louis Riel, Padraic Pearse, or Malcolm X, the intensity of the vision seems to be fired by the internal conflict coming from a culturally mixed parentage. Topiltzin's father is Mixcoatl, a Chichimec war lord from the North who snuffs out the smouldering remains of the ancient high culture of Teotihuacan and its sister communities. His mother is Chimalma, a woman of the conquered high culture. Topiltzin's father dies before he is born, and his mother dies in childbirth, so he is raised by the maternal grandparents in Tepoztlan, a center of the old Quetzalcoatl cult with strong connections to the ceremonial center of Xochicalco.[13]

Xochicalco was both a fortress and a religious center, said to have been built in the eighth and ninth centuries A.D. The time was a dark age and a period of chaos and cultural disintegration; to the south the collapse of the classic Maya civilization was taking place. Given the portraiture of the different tribes and races that remains on the entablature of the temple of the Feathered Serpent, I tend to think that Topiltzin himself redecorated and reconsecrated the temple to a vision of a united Mexico, one united under the power of the old religion common to all, the religion of Quetzalcoatl. It was a vision of a new age of gods held up right in the middle of the age of chaos; but this great vision of peace and cultural unity, much like our own vision of peace through the United Nations, failed. The rise of militarism and human sacrifice was not stopped. In failing to live out the civilizational vision of Quetzalcoatl, Topiltzin follows in the footsteps of myth and leaves Tula to make his own journey to the East. Although history is often the performance of myth, Topiltzin is a man and not a bodhisattva or transcendent god; he cannot simply sail off to the Land of Light. And so the zealous priest who suffers from a Gnostic horror of the body, a horror of the primal act of rape which brought his soul into the world and into the tragic history of Mexico, compulsively repeats that history in his own fall into sacrilegious sexuality and in his penitent rite of self-immolation. In casting himself into the fire, Topiltzin performs an act of alchemy on his own body, a rite of purification to allow the dross of the body to be cast aside so that the soul may reascend to the morning star.

With the failure of Topiltzin's prophetic movement, the age of men is ended and the age of chaos is ushered in. Here the religion of Quetzalcoatl is itself perverted into a cult of human sacrifice and, ironically, into an inspiring force for the Toltec conquest of Maya Yucatan. In this fallen age, the mirror opposite of the age of gods, there can be no question of a direct incarnation of the Feathered Serpent; instead Cortez becomes the instrument of karmic retribution, the bearded white man from the East who appears in the prophesied time of the year One Reed, Ce Acatl, and brings down the entire civilization of the warriors.

The ancient prophetic calendar says that Quetzalcoatl will return again, and that our era of the Fifth Sun is now drawing to its close and will end in earthquakes, volcanic fire, and famines.[14] The age of chaos will be consummated in chaos, and then the spiral will turn, and a new age of gods with a new sun will be established.

The myth of Quetzalcoatl is essentially a story of the conflict between body and soul, matter and spirit, earth and sun, civilization and savagery; and that is why it speaks so profoundly to our age in which civilization and savagery are so incredibly mixed. From the thermonuclear terror of the large nations to the terrorism of the nationless, the dark gods, Tezcatlipoca and Huitzilopochtli, are still with us screaming for human sacrifice. The myth of Quetzalcoatl is not once upon another time, but very much upon this time, for the fall of civilizations does not stop with us. The fall of the land before the flood, the fall of Teotihuacan, the fall of Tula, and the fall of Tenochtitlan are preludes to the fall of our own earth-destroying industrial civilization.

Poetry is the language which seeks to recall, re-call us to our senses, and poetry remains superior to history for all the reasons that Aristotle gave long ago. A scientific history can give us recorded facts, but only poetry can reveal the meaning of history in the universal truth of events. Poetry is the place where myth and history meet, the place where the collective narrative is given individual expression. In a myth the ancient prehistory of the soul is recast into the imagery and situations of more recent events. In the telling of a myth, the memory stirs and one realizes that more is being expressed than simply the story of a drunken priest's fall into sexuality. We *are* more than we *know*; therefore science never can contain us, but where the edge of knowing meets the horizon of Being is in the open landscape of myth.

Lindisfarne Mountain Retreat
Sangre de Cristo Mountains,
Christmas Eve, 1981

NOTES

1. Hans Jonas, *The Gnostic Religion* (Boston: Beacon, 1963), p. 62.

2. Da Liu, *T'ai Chi Chuan and I Ching* (New York: Harper & Row, 1972), p. 4.

3. William Irwin Thompson, *The Time Falling Bodies Take to Light: Mythology, Sexuality, and the Origins of Culture* (New York: St. Martin's, 1981), p. 112.

4. Paul D. Maclean, "New Findings Relevant to the Evolution of Psychosexual Functions of the Brain," *Journal of Nervous and Mental Disease*, Oct. 1962, p. 289. See also his *A Triune Concept of the Brain and Behavior* (Toronto: Univ. of Toronto Press, 1973).

5. See *Language and Thought in Schizophrenia*, ed. J. S. Kasanin (New York: Norton, 1964), p. 53.

6. T.S. Eliot, from "Little Gidding," *Four Quartets*, in *The Complete Poems and Plays* (New York: Harcourt Brace, 1952), p. 145.

7. See John Bierhorst, "Quetzalcoatl," in *Four Masterworks of American Indian Literature* (New York: Farrar, Straus & Giroux, 1974), p. 82, footnote 51. For students wishing to have an exact scholarly rendering of the Quetzalcoatl myth, rather than an artistic rendering, Bierhorst's is by far the most helpful.

8. Hans Jonas, op. cit., p. 122.

9. See Cyrus Gordon, *Before Columbus* (New York: Crown, 1971), and Barry Fell, *America B.C.* (New York: Quadrangle, 1977).

10. See Michael Coe, *America's First Civilization: Discovering the Olmecs* (New York: American Heritage, 1968), p. 86.

11. *The New Science of Giambattista Vico*, ed. T. Bergin and M. H. Fisch (Ithaca, New York: Cornell Univ. Press, 1970), p. 27.

12. Laurette Séjourné, *Burning Water: Thought and Religion in Ancient Mexico* (New York: Vanguard, 1956), p. 80.

13. See *Quetzalcoatl*, José Lopez-Portillo, Demetrio Sodi, and Fernando Diaz Infante (Geneva: Weber, 1980), p. 60.

14. See Miguel Leon-Portilla, *The Pre-Columbian Literatures of Mexico* (Norman, Oklahoma: Univ. of Oklahoma, 1969), p. 36; also Michael Coe, *The Maya* (London: Thames & Hudson, 1966), p. 149, and Frank Waters, *Mexico Mystique* (Sage Books, Swallow Press, 1976).

A Cycle of Poems on Quetzalcoatl

PART ONE

THE ANCIENT TEXTS

I. The Age of Gods
TAMOANCHAN

After the flood the elemental gods
Assembled under the bright dried sky.
"Shall man's life end? Or shall again
We find, ripening in man's thoughts, our food?"

Great womb of night, small seed of starlight,
Hot brilliant sun, early morning star,
Cold firmer of the shifting molten earth,
Quetzalcoatl, tiller of the land:
These were the gods assembled there.

Quetzalcoatl went to the Dead Land,
To the Lord and Lady of the Dead Land.
"These precious bones in your keep I would take."
"To make what with them, Quetzalcoatl?"
And Quetzalcoatl answered them, "The gods
Are hungry, they ask, 'Who shall live on earth?' "

The great Lord of the Dead Land spoke again:
"If you can bring breath to the still Dead Land,
Carry human breath in my cold conch shell,
Circle four times round my emerald realm,
These precious bones are yours to take away."
But the cold conch shell was solid, no sound
Could enter its unhollow coral horn.

Then Quetzalcoatl summoned boring worms
Who hollowed it; bees and hornets entered
Buzzing in the shell's inward turning spine.
Then Quetzalcoatl Ehecatl blew
And the silent Lord of the Dead Land heard.

So the cold Lord of Mictlan spoke once more:
"Very well, take them." But to his subjects,
He said, "My holy ones, tell him he must
Relinquish the bones to my ancient keep."
But Quetzalcoatl said, "I have them
Now and immortal." Then his Nahual spoke:
"Merely answer, 'I do relinquish them.' "
Quetzalcoatl spoke at once, he cried,
"I do relinquish them," but he in fact
Was ascending out of water into light.

Then truly he took the precious bones,
White bones of women, marrowed bones of men,
And wrapping them in cloth, he hurried off.
But the Lord of the Dead Land now spoke again:
"Holy ones, Quetzalcoatl is taking
The bones of men beyond our dead world's end;
Holy ones, make him a coffin, a crypt."
When Quetzalcoatl reached the morning air,
Startled by a quail, he tripped, and falling
Hit his head upon the Mictlan crypt,
Scattering man's bones to the horizon's edge.
Then the morning quail nibbled at the bones,
Making mortal the immortal marrow.
When Quetzalcoatl awoke, he cried:
"Nahual, it is undone! How will it be?"

And then at once his Nahual answered him:
"It will be undone; let be what will be."
Sadly Quetzalcoatl gathered up
The broken fragments of human bones;
To Tamoanchan he brought us in bits.
There Serpent Woman ground the bones to dust,
And in her blue jade bowl, her magic womb,
She placed them to catch Quetzalcoatl's blood
That he himself bled in sacrificial rite
From his chaste and softly perfect member.

All the gods who did penance should be named:
Evening star, firmer of the sodden mud,
Morning star, tiller of the broken earth,
Wind over water, Quetzalcoatl.

Then all the penitent gods spoke aloud:
"Born are the feeding servants of the gods,
But what will they eat? Let their food appear."
Then lightning struck the earth, Food Mountain
    cracked,
Brilliant kernels of corn by one red ant
Were brought out of the mountain to the light.

When Quetzalcoatl saw the kernels
He demanded of the ant to tell him where
To find the corn, but the red ant would not.
Over and over again he asked until
The ant in desperation shouted, "There!"
And showed the road inside Food Mountain.
Then Quetzalcoatl turned into an ant.
A black ant became Quetzalcoatl,

But it was the red ant that showed him how
To enter inside the secret mountain.
At the hold he piled up the shining corn,
Then he took it all to Tamoanchan.
There the gods chewed our brittle food for us,
And then they placed it softly on our lips
As mothers do, to make their infants strong.

Then the gods demanded, "What shall we do
With Food Mountain? Shall we just let it be?"
Immediately Quetzalcoatl
Set out to carry it away with cords,
But the mountain was too great to carry.

Then our first parents divined with kernels,
Our Oxomoco and Cipactonal
Divined and discovered that Nanahuatl,
That lightning must be the opening one
To break Food Mountain entirely apart.

But with the lightning came the rain gods too,
Blue rain gods of the north, and white rain gods
From the south; yellow rain gods from the east,
And red rain gods from the evening west.
Nanahuatl opened up Food Mountain,
But all the rain gods ate the lovely food:
White, black, red, and yellow maize, amaranth,
Beans, sage, and argemone; all the foods
Disappeared in the gods' dissolving rain.

II. The Age of Heroes
TEOTIHUACAN

This is the story the old people tell.
They say that Quetzalcoatl first came,
Not here where his pyramid still stands,
But to the farthest east at the sea's edge.
They say he appeared suddenly like wind
Over water and that is why he is called
Truly Quetzalcoatl Ehecatl.
The skin of Quetzalcoatl was white,
His hair was brown, but his full beard was red.
He wore a long robe, and sea-foam sandals
With a pointed cap of ocelot skin.

Quetzalcoatl taught us how to plant,
He brought us seeds and names for all the stars;
He knew the moon, the movements of planets,
The art of building great temples of stone,
And the fine carving of turquoise and jade.
And so it was the Toltecs his subjects
Became highly skilled; nothing was difficult
When they did it, not cast gold nor cut jade,
Nor the delicate workings in feathers.
Indeed all the crafts, all art and knowledge
Flowed out from the great Quetzalcoatl.

And there his temple stood, it was very tall,

High, exceedingly high, countless its steps,
And narrow; on each the sole of one's foot
Indeed could not be made to straightly fit.
And there apart stood his sevenfold house:
House of jadestone, house of beams, house of gold,
House of redshell, house of whiteshell, his house
Of turquoise, and his house of quetzal plumes.

And for his subjects the Toltecs no place
For them was far; such great runners they were,
They were called "Those who bend the knee all day."
And in Tollan there was a mountain called
Crying Out Mountain. There the herald stood
And cried out the laws made in Anahuac.
From there indeed it spread throughout the land;
It could be heard so quickly everywhere
That all hurried out to hear the commands
And know what Quetzalcoatl had decreed.

And in those days they had abundance there;
Cheap and plentiful were all our foods: gourds
Were huge and could be embraced in one's arms;
And maize, the ears of maize were long and heavy
As *metates*. Amaranths were like trees,
They climbed them; they truly could be climbed.
All kinds of colored cotton grew: blue, green,
Chili-red, yellow, pink, brown, purple, gold,
And even coyote-colored cotton.
All these kinds of cotton came in colors
On the bush; they did not have to dye them.
And all the birds of precious feathers dwelled
There in Anahuac: the cotinga, quetzal,

Oropendola, trogon, and spoonbill.
And all the songbirds, they too gladly sang.
And all the jade and gold was so common
That no one hoarded or thought much of it.
And cacao grew, flowery cacao grew,
In many places there were forests of cacao.
Indeed these Toltecs were very rich, wealthy.
Never were they poor, nothing was lacking
In their homes, never did they know famine.
They did not need to eat the stunted maize,
But burned it as fuel to heat their baths.

And Quetzalcoatl did penance.
He pierced his flesh with sharp maguey thorns
And secretly bathed alone at midnight
In a place called Where the Turquoise Is Washed.
Each of the priests of fire imitated him,
Also the priests of the sacred offering.
The life of Quetzalcoatl became the way
For the life of every priest in Tollan.
By Quetzalcoatl did all the customs
In Mexico become established here.

THEN IT HAPPENED THAT QUETZALCOATL
And all the Toltecs grew lax, neglectful.
And they say his face had nothing human
Left in it: aged, monstrous, and battered.

It is said he always wore a veil;
Covered was his face, even as he lay;
But much longer than his veil was his beard,
Very long, exceedingly long, and full.
And then there arrived an evil omen,
Three sorcerers came to announce Tollan
Would be destroyed: Tlacahuepan, Titlacahuan,
And Huitzilopochtli were their names.
Titlacahuan-Tezcatlipoca began
What the three sorcerers had prophesied.
First he turned himself into an old man,
A little old man with a crooked spine,
With a cracked voice, and with a white head.
Thus disguised he went to Quetzalcoatl.
When he came to the house, the bent old man,
He said to the servants, "I wish to see
The Lord Quetzalcoatl." But they said:
"Go away, little old man, the Lord is sick,
You will bother him, you will disturb him."
"No, but I will see him. I will come in."
Then the servants said: "Wait. We will tell him."
Thereupon they informed Quetzalcoatl.
They said to him: "My prince, some small old man
Has come to see you. He is like a trap,
A snare for you. When we turn him away,
He will in no way go, but staying says:
'I will see the Lord, I will see the Lord.'"
Then Quetzalcoatl said: "Let him enter,
Let him come, I have been waiting for him
For five days, even for ten, many days."
Then Tezcatlipoca stood before the Lord
Quetzalcoatl. The little bent old man

Greeted him and said, "Grandson, My Lord,
How do you feel in your body, what ails you?"
And Quetzalcoatl said: "Come here, old one.
For five days, for ten days, I have awaited you."
And then the little old man said to him:
"Grandson, how do you feel in your body?"
"Much do I ail everywhere, my body
Is all tired, my hands, my feet, all ache."
Then the little bent old man replied:
"Here is the potion, it is very good;
If you drink it, it will delight you.
Smooth and mellow, deliciously it works
To soothe within you your aching body;
You will weep, with compassion you will think
Of your own death, and where you must now go."
And Quetzalcoatl said: "Where shall I go?"
Then the bent old man said: "To Tlapalan,
To the red place of the sun where a man
Guards there; one, already aged, waits.
You two will consult with one another,
And when you return here once more you will
Again have been made like a little child."
This indeed deeply stirred Quetzalcoatl,
So the little old man spoke again: "Here,
Be cheerful and drink now of this potion."
"Old man, I will not drink it," the Lord said.
"Just drink of it. You will be in need.
Just place it in front of you as your fate;
You need only taste a little of it."
Then Quetzalcoatl tasted just a portion,
And then drank deeply. "It is very good.
What is this? No more am I sick with pain."

Then the little bent old man said to him:
"Drink of this potion deeply once again,
With it your body will gain back its strength."
And thereupon he drank the vessel down.
Quetzalcoatl became drunk; he wept,
His heart became inflamed, deeply troubled;
He could no longer forget his agony,
His mind could not move from its deep sorrow.
The sorcerer had indeed ensnared him.
It is told that the potion the old man
Gave to Quetzalcoatl was white *pulque*,
Drawn from the sap of our sacred Maguey,
The juice of the yellow-leaved Maguey plant.

AND MANY MORE EVIL OMENS APPEARED
To the Toltecs till Tollan was destroyed.
And as all these happened, Quetzalcoatl
Grieved and suffered, then he remembered
That he was to go, that he was to leave,
To abandon his city of Tollan.
Thereupon he made ready; it is said
That he had all his lordly treasures burned:
His house of gold, his house of redshells,
And all the marvelous Toltec works of craft,
The costly works of skill he buried, all.
These he hid in secret difficult places,
Inside mountains or far up in canyons.

Also the cacao trees he changed into
Mesquites. And all the lovely precious birds,
The resplendent trogons, bright cotingas,
And roseate spoonbills, these he dismissed;
He sent them on ahead, the colored birds
To the red-colored land of Tlapalan.
And when all this was done, he departed.

He set out on the road and came at first
To Cuauhtitlan. A great tree stood there,
Very tall, very thick. Quetzalcoatl
Called for his mirror and looked at himself.
"Already am I an old man." And so
He named it "The place of the old age tree."
Thereupon he stoned the tree, many stones
He threw in rage, and as they hit, they stuck.
And so even today it can be seen,
Just so has the tree continued to be:
From the foot to the top the stones extend.
Once again he came to a place to rest.
Upon a stone he sat and supported
His weight with his hands. Then Quetzalcoatl
Looked out toward Tollan and wept; as one
Sobbing violently did he weep then.
Hailstones fell as his tears; over his face
Great streams dropped and as they hit the stone,
They cut deep holes into the darkened rock.
And as Quetzalcoatl sat on the rock
His hands sank deeply as if into mud,
Also his body printed itself deep
Into the hard rock where he sat alone.
Still can you see them there, still are they there.

Hence the place is named Temacpalco.
And then he went on; he came to a place
Where there was water, a great stream flowing.
Quetzalcoatl set down stones, a true bridge;
Then he crossed over and named the place
Tepanoayan, the bridge made of stone.
And once again he set forth and arrived
At another stream called Coaapan,
"Where the serpent water is." Here wizards
Tried to turn him back, they tried to stop him.
They said: "Where are you bound? Why are you
    leaving?
Whom have you left in charge? Who shall perform
The sacred penances when you are gone?"
Then Quetzalcoatl said to the wizards:
"In no way now will it be possible
For you to stop me. I shall only go."
"But where are you going, Quetzalcoatl?"
And he answered: "I go to Tlapalan,
To learn at the place of Light and Wisdom."
"But what will you do there, Quetzalcoatl?"
And he said: "I am called, the sun calls me."
Then the wizards said to him, "Very well,
Go, but you must leave all the Toltec works
Of skill and craftsmanship, all the great arts."
Then Quetzalcoatl left there all the arts,
The casting of gold, the cutting of jade,
The sculpturing in turquoise, the carving
Of wood, the placing of feathers, the art
Of the scribe's painted stories, all were stripped,
All were stolen, all were taken from him.
When this was done Quetzalcoatl scattered
His jewels into the water and watched

46

As they were swept away, and so he named
The place Cozcaapan, "Jewels in Water";
But now it is called Coaapan,
"The place where the Serpent Water is."

And then Quetzalcoatl moved on and came
To the place of Cochtocan, "Where he sleeps."
And there another wizard came to him:
"Where are you going, Quetzalcoatl?"
And he answered him: "To Tlapalan,
I go now to learn at the place of Light."
Then the wizard said to him: "It is well,
But drink this which I have concocted here."
But Quetzalcoatl said: "No, in no way
Can I drink it, not even in a taste."
Then once again the wizard said to him:
"It cannot be that neither do you drink
Nor taste of it. No one do I except,
None do I excuse, none do I let pass.
All must drink, and drinking, become thus drunk."
Then Quetzalcoatl drank it through a reed,
And quickly he fell asleep in the road.
He lay there snoring, loud was his snoring
That it could be heard echoing back at him.
When he awoke he looked from side to side,
He looked at himself and arranged his hair.
And then he named the place Cochtocan,
"The place where one falls into deep sleeping."

Quetzalcoatl rose and again set forth.
To Popocatepetl and Iztactepetl;
There in the mountain pass he slowly climbed
With his troop of hunchbacks and dwarves,

47

His company of servants. And as they climbed
It snowed heavily and cold upon them.
There they froze, there they all died of the cold.
And Quetzalcoatl grieved, he wept and sang
Laments to himself. Greatly did he weep.
In the distance he saw another white mountain,
Poyauhtecatl. Again he set forth.
He passed by everywhere, passing villages,
Everywhere he left signs by which he is known.
In one place he gamboled on a mountain,
Swung down cliffs on ropes of Maguey fibres.
In one place he built a ball court of stone,
And at the middle line he dug a trench.
Elsewhere he shot himself like an arrow
Passing through the heart of the cotton tree.
And in another place he built underground
A house and called it Mictlan, Of the Dead.
And elsewhere he set in place a huge stone;
One could move it with his little finger;
From side to side it would teeter and rock,
But when many pushed it, it would not move.
And still many other things did he do
Everywhere in the towns and villages.
And everywhere he went he gave out names,
Truly he gave names to all the mountains.
And when this was done, he came to the sea.
And there he wove reeds into serpents to make
A raft, a raft of serpents for his boat.
And then he set off and was swept away
By wind over water, and no one knows
The way he came at last to Tlapalan.

III. The Age of Men
TULA

In the year 1 Reed, it is said,
In the time of the morning star,
It is told that Topiltzin,
Ce Acatl Quetzalcoatl,
Our Noble Prince, our Priest, was born.

Chimalma was his mother's name,
And they say this was the manner
In which Quetzalcoatl came
God-like into his mother's womb:
Chimalma swallowed an emerald.

War Lord, his father, Mixcoatl,
Was killed and buried in the sand;
Upon his birth his mother died.

There came the years 2 Flint, 3 House,
4 Rabbit, 5 Reed, 6 Flint,
7 House, 8 Rabbit, 9 Reed.
In 9 Reed Quetzalcoatl
Asked about his absent father:
"I wish to see my father's face."
"He is dead. There is he buried."
Quetzalcoatl went at once
To search the earth, to turn the sand.
He brought the bones into the light,

And at the shrine of Quilaztli,
He prayed and buried them again.

In the year 2 Rabbit it was
Quetzalcoatl came to stay
For four years in Tulancingo.
There he built his house of penance,
His house of turquoise, house of beams.
From there he went through Cuextlan;
In that place he crossed a river
With a bridge of his own making,
All of stone, they say, still it stands.
In the year 5 House the Toltecs
Came and asked Quetzalcoatl
To become their king, to rule them
In Tula as their sacred Priest.

In the year 2 Reed he built his house,
House of penance, house of prayer.
He built his house as four: a house
Of turquoise, a house of whiteshell,
Redshell, and of precious feathers.
There he worshipped, there he fasted.
Even at midnight he went down
To the stream called Edge of Water,
There in the dark where the moss was.
Of jade and maguey were the thorns
He set in penance in his flesh.
On the summit of Xicocotl,
On Tzincoc, on Nonohualca,
Only his prayers could be heard.
Fumed with incense, sacred copal,

Were his thorns of turquoise, of jade.
And the offerings that he made
Were never men, but only snakes,
Birds, butterflies in sacrifice.
They say he sent up his prayers
To the deep heart of the sky,
And they knew that he was crying
Out to the place of Duality
Beyond the gods' ninefold heavens.
And thus they knew, those who dwelt there,
That he called upon them, humbly
And contritely, he prayed to them.

And in his time he discovered
Great riches: gold, silver, turquoise,
Jadestone, redshell, whiteshell, feathers,
Plumes of quetzal, of cotinga,
Blue heron, roseate spoonbill,
Trogon, and the oropendola.
And cacao, he discovered cacao
Of many colors, and cottons
Of all colors like birds' feathers.
Truly in his time he was great
In all the arts; the simple pot
From which he ate and drank could hold
Painted gods in the earthenware.
Also in his time he began
His great temple, our pyramid.
He lifted its serpent pillars
To the sky, but he did not stay
To finish it before he went
Beyond our mountains to the sea.

In the time he lived he did not
Show himself in public, but dwelled
Deep within his house, protected.
In every room there were pages,
And his guarded room was the last.
Many times sorcerers had tried
To force our Quetzalcoatl
Into making offerings of
Men, of human sacrifice,
But never would he give consent
For he loved his Toltec subjects.
Always he would offer only
Rites of snakes, birds, and butterflies.
So it is told he angered them,
The sorcerers, and they conspired
To find the way to make him flee.

And this is how they say he left,
How Quetzalcoatl fled the land.
When he refused to sacrifice
His beloved Toltec subjects,
The sorcerers assembled, they
Whose names are Tezcatlipoca,
Ihuimecatl, and Toltecatl.
"He must leave his city, let us
Corrupt him, let us make *pulque*,
So that, drunk, he will no longer
Perform his priestly sacraments."
Then Tezcatlipoca said: "I,
I say we give him his body
To see in the smoking mirror."

But who can say how or in what
Manner they conspired to act?
Tezcatlipoca went there first,
Carrying the smoking mirror
Concealed in a soft wrapping.
And when Tezcatlipoca came
Before the pages of the house,
He said: "Announce to the Priest, say,
'Lord, a servant has come to show
You your body, that you may see.'"
The pages went into the house;
They stood before the Lord who said:
"What is this? What body of mine
Can he bring? Examine it first,
Only then may you let him in."
But Tezcatlipoca would not
Permit them to see his mirror.
"I, only I will show the Priest. .
Tell him no other is allowed."
Then the pages informed their Lord:
"He refuses now to show it,
He insists that only he can
Himself show your body to you."
And then Quetzalcoatl said:
"Let him come in, grandfather page."
Then Tezcatlipoca entered,
And greeted him, saying: "My son,
Priest, 1 Reed Quetzalcoatl,
Lord, I have come to salute you
And to show you your body."
Quetzalcoatl said to him:
"You have taken great pains, Old One.

From what great distance do you come,
And what is this body of mine?"
Then Tezcatlipoca answered:
"My son, Priest, I am your servant
Come from your Mount Nonohualca.
May it please you to see your body."
And then Tezcatlipoca stretched
And held out the darkening mirror:
"Behold your body. Envision
In obsidian your true form.
It is here in this glass you shall
Appear in the smoke that mirrors."
When he looked into the mirror,
Quetzalcoatl was afraid:
"If my subjects were to see me,
They would run in horror."
For he saw his eyelids swollen,
The eyes sunken, the face bilious,
Green and distended out of shape.
"Never shall my subjects see me thus;
I will stay in my house alone."

Tezcatlipoca left the house
And went back to the sorcerers.
Ihuimecatl said: "Let us mock
Quetzalcoatl; let the artist
Coyotlinahual be the one."
Then the sorcerers informed him,
Told him that he must be the one
To taunt the Priest with skillful craft.
The artist Coyotlinahual
Agreed at once to work his art:

"I shall see Quetzalcoatl."
He went at once and to the Lord
He shouted out in the courtyard:
"My son, I say, come out, be seen!
I will dress you for all to see."
Coyotlinahual went to work.
First he made the Lord's quetzal plumes,
Then he made him his turquoise mask,
With red stone for the mouth, yellow
For the forehead, then serpent's teeth
And a beard of cotinga plumes.
And when he had arranged the mask
For our Lord Quetzalcoatl,
He gave him a mirror to see.
And Quetzalcoatl greatly
Admired himself and felt transformed;
At once he abandoned his refuge
In procession for all to see.

The artist Coyotlinahual
Went back to Ihuimecatl.
"I have lured Quetzalcoatl
Out of his house. He stands exposed."
"It is well," said Ihuimecatl,
And then he found Toltecatl
And together they took the road
And traveled to the distant place
Where Onions are Washed. There they lodged
With the old harvestman, Mixtla,
The keeper of Toltec Mountain.
There they began to blend a stew
Of herbs, tomatoes, hot peppers,

Young corn, red onions, and black beans.
This they cooked for several days,
And with maguey they made *pulque*.
It was they too who discovered
The wild honeycombs, and with these
They made a new kind of *pulque*.
And then with the stew and the *pulque*
They returned to Tula to tempt
Our Noble Prince, our Sacred Priest.

When they arrived the guards refused
To let them enter; two and three
Times they were stopped and turned away.
At last they were asked for their home.
"There beyond is our land, see it!,
The Priests' Mountain, Toltec Mountain."
When Quetzalcoatl overheard
The words of the two sorcerers
He told his guards, "Let them enter."
Quickly they entered and greeted him
And offered him the stew of herbs.
And when he had eaten, they gave
The *pulque* to him for his drink.
"No, I cannot drink it. I abstain.
Does it take away the senses?
Is it deadly?" Then they answered:
"Merely with the fingertip, taste
Only the tiniest amount.
It is strong. It is newly made."
With merely his small fingertip
Quetzalcoatl tasted it,
And finding it good, then he said:

"I would drink more, Grandfather, three
More draughts." But the sorcerers answered:
"Four more shall you drink, only four."
Thus they gave him even his fifth,
Saying: "This is your sacrament."

When Quetzalcoatl had drunk,
They served all his pages, they too
Took their five draughts and fell down drunk.
Then the sorcerers turned and said:
"Quetzalcoatl, we have songs,
My son, may it please you to sing:

> House of quetzal, of quetzal,
> Of zacuan, of redshell,
> I leave thee! An ya!"

Then with joy, Quetzalcoatl
Cried: "Bring me my elder sister,
Quetzalpetlatl. Now may we
Drink, and sing, and sleep together."

Alone on Mount Nonohualca
The pure lady prayed and fasted.
There the pages found her and said:
"Penitent Lady, my daughter,
We have come commanded to take
You back to Quetzalcoatl;
The Priest awaits you in his house.
Now you must go to be with him."
"Then let us go, Grandfather Page."
Down from the mountain to the house
The Lady came and sat by him,
Our Noble Prince, our Sacred Priest.

There she was given the *pulque,*
And she took her four draughts, even
Her fifth. Thus Ihuimecatl
And Toltecatl made both them drunk.
Then to her, Quetzalpetlatl,
They chanted together this song:

> *Where now is your home,*
> *My sister, my Quetzalpetlatl?*
> *Oh it's here in your bottle*
> *With the drunk Quetzalcoatl.*
> *Ayn ya! ynya yn ye an!*

Now that they were drunk, no longer
Did they fast, no longer did they
Pierce their flesh with maguey thorns;
Not down to the river nor alone
At dawn on mountains did they pray.
This dawn when they awoke they grieved,
Heavy indeed were their spirits.

Then Quetzalcoatl composed
His lament for leaving Tula.

> *No more!*
> *No more will the days*
> *Be counted in my house.*
> *I awaken to the East.*
> *From earth, from flesh,*
> *From pain and burning,*
> *I quickly depart.*
> *No more shall I thrive here.*

Then he sang yet another song.

> *My mother of the earth,*
> *She will nurse me no more.*
> *She of the Serpent Skirt,*
> *She will hold me no more.*
> *Ah! the holy one!*
> *I, her child, alone*
> *Am weeping, iya ye an!*

The songs made all the pages sad;
They too wept and began to sing:

> *No more can we*
> *delight in him,*
> *Our noble one,*
> *Quetzalcoatl.*
> *No more your crown;*
> *the bleeding thorns*
> *are broken now.*
> *We mourn for him,*
> *We weep and cry.*

When the lament of the pages
Was ended, Quetzalcoatl
Spoke to them: "Grandfather, enough!
Now I must go from this city;
Give the command to carve at once
A funeral urn large enough
To hold my suspended body."
Quickly the Toltecs crafted it,
And when it was finished, placed
The Priest in trance within the crypt.

But he lay for only four days
In his skillfully crafted urn.
"Enough, Grandfather, we will go!"
"But everywhere conceal the things
Created from our Toltec arts:
Our joy, our beauty, and our wealth;
Hide all the treasure, all of it."
And this the pages did; they hid
All at the Edge of the Water,
Where the green water moss was,
The place where Quetzalcoatl
Used to bathe alone at midnight.
When the pages had finished this,
He called them once more together,
And weeping over them, he left;
For Tlillan Tlapallan, he searched,
The Black Land, the Red Land, he sought.

Quetzalcoatl traveled far,
But no place was pleasing to him.
And everywhere he went, he wept.
Finally in the year 1 Reed
He reached the shore, the water's edge.
There they say he wept and once more
Put on his quetzal plumes, his mask;
And when he was thus attired
In all his priestly robes, he set
Himself on fire, surrendering
In silence to the burning flames.
They say also that as he burned
His ashes rose into the air,
And all the precious birds were seen:

Roseate spoonbill, cotinga,
Trogon, white and yellow parrot,
Blue heron and scarlet macaw;
All rose with his ashes to the sky.
And when all the ashes were gone,
The heart and the innermost part
Of the precious quetzal penis
Rose upward to the morning star.

Such was the life of him who was
Truly called Quetzalcoatl.
He was born in 1 Reed; he died
In 1 Reed. Now it is finished,
In the time, in the year, 1 Reed.

 PART TWO

THE THEME IN VARIATION

I. Topiltzin's Address
At Xochicalco

War Lord, my father, Mixcoatl,
Smashed the last remaining ashes
Of greatest Teotihuacan.
His crude feet crushed quetzal feathers
As he trod upon the slaughtered priests—
Skull stones that paved a sacred street
At the pyramid of the sun.

Priestess, my mother stood among
The gods' pure women in a group
Taken from the broken temple.
The Chichimec conqueror came
Grinning as he crushed heads in dirt.
Lovely to him was the language
Of their ancient laments, except
The silent one with still blue eyes.
Driven to rage by the alien
Lineage of her Atlantic eyes,
He thrust his hand into her robe,
And with twisting fist, the savage
Took her by shock and maiden hair,
Running in shame against herself,
To the steps of the pyramid.
Her blood and his seed stained the rock
Where once the great Lord of Tollan
Called down the laws to Anahuac.

My mother's blue eyes I carry
In the body of my father:
Eyes open from the feathered sky,
Body closed from the serpent's earth.
I have inherited two Lands,
But I shall pass on only one.
One Mexico for Zapotec,
Mixtec, Quiché, Toltec, Maya.
Within the folds of the feathered
Serpent all will be held in peace,
As round this temple the serpent
Enfolds the races of the world.
No more shall there be holy wars
Or human sacrifice. Return!
Hear again the song of Tollan
In the sun and the morning star.

II. Meditation
on Mount Nonohualca

Nahual: You thrust these thorns into your skin
To bring the body to a point.
The separate edges of a blade,
Body and mind can only come
Together in a point. Sharp pain
Is a body transformed to mind.
If you can watch your pain as I
With lid-less nahual eyes watch you,
You can be free to watch your death
To find we are a single mind.
Thus does the bird take up the snake
From trunk to broken-open sky.

Body can endlessly demand
New satisfactions of its needs.
It cries for food, and so you fast;
It cries for sleep, you stay awake;
It cries for peace, you give it pain.
When the leaves are full, who can see
The roots, the branches, or the tree?

Topiltzin: I begin now to understand:
Anahuac, I am not other
But only am another hand
On your single sunlit body.

Both priest and warrior take pain
And lift it to a way of life,
For what one fears, one must inflict.
But, Mexico, you have made death
Your only vital sacrament.
The thorns are larger that you thrust
In self-inflicted history.

Everything I have built will fall;
I and this mountain cannot be
More than the people or the land.
I see the Toltecs sacrifice
Men in Quetzalcoatl's name,
And conquer until conquerors
Come crossing from the East again.
Two races meet violently
In me. Another two will wed
In blood to breed a hard third race:
Black oceans under earth are turned
Like open graves into the air;
Cities beyond counting cover
The soil like scabs and running sores.
Then earth cracks and volcanoes break,
And those who choked the earth are choked,
Those who brought the dead seas up, slide
Down with their cities to the sea.

The blood drenched flesh upon my bones
Is bound like cloth upon a torch.
Since birth I have been burning years,
What else is left but lift the torch
To clear a space with planting fire?

III. Morning in Tula

So this is my body:
Wet blood and female slime
Fermenting on my groin,
Wet seed upon your hair.
Do we come from the sea
That thus we smell like fish?

Nights when we slept chastely
Were subtle bodies' love;
Our least alighting touch
Was cooling as blue jade.
Far deeper than the womb,
Our love was in the spine,
Trunk of the world's tree.
Above body's mud, we climbed
Becoming Quetzal birds.
On top the trees in light,
We were always, only
Alive in sunlit air.
Now this wet, matted hair,
This dripping genital swamp.
Like newborn men, I slide
Down mothers' thighs in scum.

I on this fallen earth
Endure another fall.
Back to the lunar womb,
I seek my father sun.
My head must thrust again,
Returning to the rank,
Salt, wet, corroding sea.

IV. Quetzalpetlatl

I heard no sound, footstep or branch,
But because the birds stopped singing,
I too looked up. You did not speak.
Alone in the clearing by the huts,
You looked at me with pale blue eyes;
I had not seen blue eyes before.
Pale clouds for skin, blue birds for eyes,
You stared at me and no one else.
That very night my woman's time
Turned inside out of me; my breasts
Hurt, throbbing within my tightened skin.
All night my eyes stared at the thatch
And one bright star inside the crack.
Why, being so strange, should you seem
So familiar? As if I dreamed
Pale clouds for skin, blue birds for eyes.

You brought blue jade and said it came
In lightning from the morning star.
Man's flesh was hot, you said, but gods
Had flesh of jade, sunlight for blood.
But when you offered me the stone,
I quietly touched your cold white hand.

Praying with jade conjured with copal,
You called upon abandoned gods
Who had in turn abandoned us
Before the First Sun's burning flood.
You cried aloud to damaged skies;
I heard the thunder, the shaking earth
Echoing in my empty womb.
Of all the strange prayers you taught me
When you took me to your turquoise house,
Strangest were the prayers you taught
When you took me to your turquoise bed.
On birds' feathers we slept above
The spider's snare, the scorpion's sting,
But late last night I finally saw
Blue jade within your naked skin.
Now wet upon my glistening hair
Your seed brightens from the morning star.
The gods you call are not in floods,
Broken worlds or distant stars.
Everything is always here,
What is not, is not anywhere.
We are the naked feet of gods
Who tread the lovely brutal earth.
Anointed now I prophesy:
Our noble prince shall found a line
Of prophets to the end of time;
Then from your sky spent wandering,
Drawn to our dark earth again,
You'll find your body in demanding birth.

Set in Trump Mediaeval
and Oracle phototypes
by A & B Typesetters
Concord, New Hampshire

Production coordination by
W.S. Konecky Associates
New York City

Designed at the Lindisfarne Press